NLP for Fast W(
How to Lose Weight with Neuro-Linguistic Programming Techniques: Program Your Weight Loss Success NOW!

SECOND REVISED EDITION (SEPTEMBER 2014)

By James Adler

Copyright James Adler© 2014

www.facebook.com/HolisticWellnessBooks

All rights reserved. No part of this publication may be reproduced, stored in a retrieval system, or transmitted, in any form or by any means, electronic, mechanical, photocopying, recording or otherwise, without the prior written permission of the author and the publishers.

The scanning, uploading, and distribution of this book via the Internet or via any other means without the permission of the author is illegal and punishable by law. Please purchase only authorized electronic editions, and do not participate in or encourage electronic piracy of copyrighted materials.

INTRODUCTION Why Diets Don't Work...4

CHAPTER 1 Practical NLP for Busy People...6

CHAPTER 2 Mind Over Matter...13

CHAPTER 3 NLP During Your Weight Loss Program...35

CHAPTER 4 Simple NLP Techniques to Maintain Your Weight Loss Success...63

CONCLUSION How to Take Positive and Purposeful Action Today...69

INTRODUCTION

It is my desire that this book will give you a general understanding of Neuro-Linguistic Programming and how you can use this method of study to lose weight and keep it off. Many people have little knowledge about this powerful discipline that allows you to change how you think. You will be empowered to achieve your weight loss goals.

This book introduces ideas and presents techniques exclusive to NLP. Neuro-linguistic Programming is sometimes referred to as "the study of success," and has assisted many people in reaching virtually any goal. It helped me to lose weight and keep it off. I know that it will assist you as well.

Most diet and exercise plans do not work because they do not utilize any techniques to change your mindset. The mind is where will power and motivation start. NLP techniques are centrally focused on the way that thought influences behavior. NLP makes it is possible to stay focused and motivated in order to achieve weight loss and, most importantly, to maintain it.

CHAPTER 1 PRACTICAL NLP FOR A BUSY PERSON IN THE 21ST CENTURY

Are you sick of the way that circumstances in your life have turned out, or even just the way that things are going? I have been there. I had goals, but would always fall short. A recurring question in the back of my mind was always, "There are others out there who are always winning; how can I win too?" I found out that the only thing I needed to do was change the way I looked at things, change the process that I used to deal with what happens. Success is not found in *what* happens to you, it is found in the way that you *handle* what happens. Find out how someone has achieved success and copy the techniques that they used to handle their circumstances. Neuro-linguistic Programming is just that simple.

Neuro-linguistic Programming has been proven to work for people who are looking to successfully solve a number of problems that they have encountered in life. Stress, anxiety, depression, phobias, addictions, relationship issues, difficulty with weight as experienced in eating disorders, and many other difficulties have been "cured" using Neuro-linguistic Programming strategies and techniques. The symptoms of these problems are not what need to be addressed. We need to determine how we ended up in these situations and change what steps we took to get there.

Neuro-linguistic Programming is not the study of *what* you think. It is the study of *how* you think. NLP looks into the process of thought and feeling. Practicing NLP techniques will change your behavior, which in turn, will change your outcome. It is easy to say, "Think positively," but without the tools to be able to do so, it is easier said than done. That is exactly what Neuro-linguistic Programming provided me with, the tools to think optimistically and confidently.

NLP looks at the connections linking how we think (neuro), communicate (linguistic) and the repetitions of our emotions and behaviors (programs). It is important to note the different parts of the terms in order to get the most out of the process.

The term "neuro" is referring to your neurological system. We come in contact with the world using the five senses. The information gathered through these senses is then communicated into conscious and unconscious thought. These thoughts trigger the neurological system which controls our bodily processes, behaviors, and sentiments.

"Linguistic" describes the way we employ language to understand the world around us, acquire and comprehend what happens to us in life, and the process in which we transfer that information to others.

The word "programming" is used to describe how we decipher, code, and store our experiences. Your personal programming consists of your internal processes and strategies (thinking patterns) that you use to make decisions, solve problems, learn, evaluate, and get results. NLP shows us how to recode our experiences and restructure our internal programming so that we can get the outcomes that we desire.

Modelling behavior is a key element of Neuro-linguistic Programming. The belief is that if one person can achieve success by following certain mental steps, then anyone can. Very simply, you ask someone who has attained success how they did it. You observe and listen to what they tell you. You use the answers as tools to apply to your own situation and follow the steps that they took. Questions like how they prepared for a certain situation or how they bounced back when having a set-back are examples that will help you in your circumstance.

Neuro-linguistic Programming is a toolkit full of useful techniques that you can use to study and attain success. There are hundreds of different techniques for different personalities and circumstances. They are all intended to help people succeed. It is usually recommended to learn about NLP through detailed books, from NLP practitioners and therapists, or take a seminar with a coach. The world of Neuro-linguistic Programming is vast. The more I studied, the more that there was to learn. The techniques can be used in any circumstance, for anyone. The possibilities of their results are endless.

Reaching and maintaining a healthy weight can be a difficult thing for some people to do. Failure leads to disappointment and shame. Sometimes these feelings lead to even more weight gain through over-eating or just lack of motivation to exercise. Eating disorders are another major hurdle to overcome in weight loss. You also need will power to exercise and resist the temptation to eat too much. I know I did. I successfully achieved a weight loss of thirty pounds and have continued to keep it off for the last five years, all by changing how I think. The understanding and use of Neuro-linguistic Programming strategies helped me and can help you as well.

Having a good comprehension of Neuro-linguistic Programming and its methods can lead success to every area of life. I will share with you how it helped me to achieve my goal of losing weight and maintaining that weight loss through a healthy diet and exercise.

CHAPTER 2: MIND OVER MATTER. GETTING STARTED ON NLP

Losing weight and keeping it off was always difficult for me. I knew *what* I needed to do. I just did not know *how* to mentally take steps to get there. A change of thinking and attitude toward myself, food, and exercise was required. I did not know how to make that adjustment. That is where Neuro-linguistic Programming came in. It gave me the tools that I needed in order to realize my goal by altering my thought processes and my feelings toward myself and food. I was able to lose weight and keep it off.

NLP is not a magic cure, but it will help you to reach your weight loss goals by changing the way that you think. In NLP we are given tools that enable us to be successful. Now, you are not going to lose weight with the power of your mind, but you will be able to change thoughts and behaviors that might hinder your weight loss. You will also develop attitudes and behaviors that will propel you in the right direction down the path to health! Our minds are very powerful and so is our imagination. Neuro-linguistic Programming helps us to use both to their full potential, assisting us in achieving and maintaining our goals.

With NLP, you can learn how to: make unhealthy habits undesirable and make heathy ones more desirable. You will be able to get rid of beliefs that may have kept you from your fitness goals and replace them with ones that will allow you to achieve healthy weight loss more easily.

Neuro-linguistic Programming tricks the mind into changing the way that it reacts to both unhealthy and healthy foods. You can instill new, positive behaviors while negating old, self-destructive behavior. Our minds can get rid of previously limiting beliefs and be programmed with new ones. How exciting!

How does this work? Well, NLP fools your mind into changing its response to certain stimuli. NLP also tricks the brain into believing things that we may not have thought to be true in the past. If you want a different mindset, NLP is your answer. Many people fail when it comes to losing weight and keeping it off. The most common reason for this is a negative or improper mind set. Here is some insight as to how our brains react to NLP methods when we first start to practice them. For example:

- The prefrontal cortex is the area of the brain that tells your body to pretend as if the healthy food you are consuming is delicious.

- Then the insula informs you that this is false. It brings up the same distasteful sensory information that you usually experience when eating health food.

- All of the sudden, your temporal and parietal lobes are acting strange. They are showing reflexive signs of pleasure!

- Now, the amygdala is sending out weak signals of pleasure to the other parts of the brain. These faint, pleasurable emotions signal the other areas to produce emotion. The better you fake it, the stronger you make it!

- Next, the hippocampus pairs up the feelings of pleasure with process of eating the healthy food. It tells the insula that you are in fact eating healthy food.

- This confirmation by the hippocampus changes the information in the insula. The insula now stores the new feelings connected to the healthy food and stores them away for future reference. You now have a new point of reference and new pathways in the brain!

The more we repeat these sorts of processes, the more feelings and ideas we can change. We can build many of new pathways in the brain. We can strengthen the effect of the NLP techniques by using them consistently. Soon enough, we will subconsciously have new ideas, emotions, and behaviors that will ensure our weight loss success.

Here are five tips that will help you to get the most out of NLP, enabling you to get the most out of your weight loss journey:

1. Model excellence. See what others who were/are successful in achieving weight loss have done or are doing. Choose a source that you trust; an example who's opinion that you respect. Do your research! In NLP we are taught that if another person can achieve a goal, we can too. Read and learn as much as possible about the person and technique that you are going to model. This will help you before you begin your program, and along the way!

2. Attitude is key! We need to take the time to prepare ourselves and set up a good foundation before starting out on our quest to achieve a goal. Before starting a new lifestyle we have to make sure that our outlook is positive, yet

realistic. Realize that you will not know everything before you start. You will hit road blocks along the way. You will have to move past obstacles. Just know above all else that you can do this! See yourself already fully engaged in your new lifestyle. Attitude is everything.

3. Be inquisitive and allow room for misunderstandings. You are not going to know everything ahead of time. Wondering about things (details or the big picture) will propel you to work harder to see how the process is going to play out. Curiosity will also push you to investigate and learn more about the NLP and how it benefits healthy eating and exercise. Misunderstandings will arise and at times you will get confused. This is ok, and can actually be quite beneficial. You will be pulled out of your comfort zone and forced into new ways of behaving and thinking.

4. Transformation is important. You will have to change. People want change in their lives but are unwilling to alter themselves and their

behaviors. NLP techniques will help you to modify your thought processes and get rid of past behavior that may have been leading you down a path that you did not want to be on. By utilizing NLP techniques, you can put the past behind you, including mistakes and negative thought processes. You can start to anticipate positive outcomes. Embrace the transformations and modifications with open arms.

5. Make the most of the journey by having a blast! Your road to weight loss does not just end in one concrete location. There are many twists and turns on the path. With so many outcomes and so many different avenues that will help you achieve weight loss, you might as well choose the fun road, instead of the high road. It has been proven that people stick with programs that are enjoyable, and what is more enjoyable than FUN? Be serious about losing weight, but learn to laugh at yourself. Take the journey seriously, but taking yourself too

seriously may sabotage your program! Enjoy the process!

The first thing I did when I began down the road to successful weight loss was to make sure that I had plenty of motivation. Motivation is a driving force in achieving any goal. We all know it definitely takes motivation to get to the gym and work out. Exercise is a large part of the solution to staying healthy and losing weight. I took certain steps using a visualization technique that helped to encourage my desire to work out and reach my goal. I had to be enthusiastic about starting my journey and this technique helped me to do so. It can help you as well!

VISUALIZATION TECHNIQUE

Step 1- Take the time to relax. Breathe deeply and unwind without distraction. Close your eyes and stand up.

Step 2- Allow yourself to think about a time in the imminent future when you will be delighted with yourself because you have been going to the gym and exercising on a regular basis.

Step 3- Visualize as an outsider how you will look when you have been working out consistently. How do you appear physically? Are you the size you want to be? You are toned and looking confident and happy. In your mind envision every detail of your new appearance.

Step 4- Take an actual step forward and picture yourself stepping into your new self. You will now be visualizing everything through your own eyes, this "new you." You are physically fit and feeling amazing.

Step 5- Be conscious of how spectacular it feels to be in shape. Realize how much energy and motivation you have now that you have achieved success. What does it feel like to be in your healthy, fit body?

Step 6- What are you noticing with your five senses? What emotional feelings are you experiencing? Turn these feelings up, like an emotional volume control. Feel them to the extreme. Allow yourself to feel incredible in the most intense way while you visualize yourself going to the gym or getting ready to work out. Revel in this moment for as long as possible.

Step 7- Hold on to those emotions as you come back to your current self and open your eyes.

When I directed my thoughts in a certain way I was able to motivate myself to exercise. This is because the central nervous system does not recognize a real event or an imagined event as dissimilar. What you visualize in your mind can be more powerful than what you tell yourself. The imagination is more influential than the conscious psyche.

BELIEF CREATION

Do you feel like you are stuck in your old belief system regarding your fitness or weight loss goals? Well, you can change that despite what you may think. It is easy to do. We are not stuck in our thinking. We need to make new beliefs and give ourselves more options and flexibility. Otherwise, our outcome will never change. You can never get something that you have never had by doing the same things you have always done.

An example of my own use of Belief Creation had to do with my own physical fitness, or should I say lack thereof. I created the belief that I could get through a rigorous workout without too much effort... and without dying of course. When I began to honestly believe it, guess what? I WAS ABLE TO DO IT! Just believing that I could get through a super intense workout made it easy for me to make progress and accomplish something I had never done before. My negative, self-sabotaging beliefs had been holding me back!

Practice creating small beliefs first. This will enable you to erase doubt about the fact that this kind of technique will work at all. Beliefs cannot be created when there is uncertainty involved. The more that you see this method work, the greater the impact your newly created beliefs.

Here is an easy way to integrate Belief Creation, step by step, into your weight loss program:

1. Focus on something that you truly believe. Make sure that it is something you sincerely know to be factual. It could be as simple as, "The world is round." Whatever belief you choose, visualize it. What image do you see? Where is the location of the image? Centered? Left? Right? Is it near or far in your mind's eye? Is there any self-talk associated with this image,

any sounds? After analyzing and noting these things, focus your thoughts on something else. It could be anything: laundry, the rain, your recently stubbed toe, etc. You can also let your brain relax and think about nothing.

2. Ok, now it is time to choose a belief that you do not truly believe in. Choosing a belief that you do not really care if it is true or false may be most helpful. Follow the questioning process as in step one, while visualizing this belief.

3. Now that you have figured out where the two visualizations of these ideas/beliefs are, pick a belief that you would like to realize as truth. For example, "Healthy, alkaline foods are delicious." Bring up this belief in your mind's eye. Take note of where the location is of this image. First, shift this newfound belief into the same spot where you had the belief that you do not really care about. Next, move the new belief to the same spot that you placed your validated belief. If you have any words (self-talk) or sounds associated with the new belief, say them

over and over to yourself as you park the picture into the validated idea position.

Some issues that you may encounter:

- The new picture/image will not shift into a new position. All that you must do to fix this problem is to put the picture far into the distance, away from you, until it is almost out of sight. When it is almost too small to see, bring it back close to you. Place it where it should be, in the same spot that you hold the belief that you see as fact.

If the picture you hold in regard to your freshly created belief keeps moving back to where it was when you originally came up with it, you can:

- Make a sound in your head to signal the movement of the image to its new "believed" spot.

- Picture yourself putting glue on the back of the picture and stick it into its new position.

- Imagine yourself staple-gunning or nailing the image where you want it to stay.

- Envision any way that you would keep something in a relocated spot in real life, and fix your image using that method.

- Note: make sure that all images are equal size, especially the believed image and the newly created belief image.

Make sure that your new belief will work. You can do this by letting your mind attach to a different thought, or just let it relax and go blank for a bit. Now, think about the belief that you created. What position did it automatically move to? Is it the same size as the others? Does your self-talk believe it to be true?

If it is still not working, keep doing the exercise over and over, from start to finish, until it works. This method is a simple and effective way to create a new belief that will get your weight loss program off to a great start.

MAPPING ACROSS

When we begin any sort of a new program in our lives, it is sometimes important for us to change our view of certain things. If we decide that something makes us happy, or that certain foods are delicious, it makes our new lifestyle much easier to adopt and adapt to. In my life, I needed to change the way that I felt about raw, green vegetables or I was not going to get far in my healthy weight loss venture. I needed to feel the same way for vegetables that I did for French fries and tortilla chips! Sound impossible? It is not. This method can also work for addictions or compulsions, such as a sugar addiction. Here is how you can see things differently and experience a fondness for things that you may have never thought to be possible:

1. Figure out exactly what idea you would like to alter. You will need to mentally put yourself directly into this situation. Let us go back to my example. In my mind I was seated in front of a huge table full of dark, green, raw vegetables. I could see them, smell them, and hear the awful crunching noise that they made in my mouth. YUCK! I took detailed notes of the sights, sounds, and smells associated with the situation. When you write down what you notice in your situation, do not be afraid to have too many details. Also, take note of where the mental image is playing out in your mind. Where is it, how bright is it, and how large is it?

2. Next, picture yourself in a situation that brings a large amount of pleasure or joy. It could also be a situation that you disgusts you. If you are addicted to ice cream and want to be rid of that feeling, visualize a sewer or something revolting. To make it easy for myself, I envisioned sitting in front of a large dessert tray, filled with every sweet, delicious cake,

cookie, and pastry I could imagine. I noted every detail, as in the first step, and relished in the moment!

3. You want to note the differences in the situations. What answers to the questions that you asked yourself are almost opposite? You may only find a couple, but these are very important. It could be as simple as one scenario playing out in color and the other in black and white.

4. Now, you want to use at least one of the differences and apply it to the first situation (the feeling that you want to change or get rid of). For instance, in my first visualization the size was rather small, and the room was cold and dank. The colors were pretty dull. In the second, it was a large scene in a warm room full of color and lovely smells. All I had to do was visualize myself sitting in front of the vegetables and switch up certain aspects of the scene. I made the visualization huge, imagined the room warm and colorful, and full of delicious

smells. I would repeat this over and over, taking breaks after each switch. Eventually, I did not have to consciously make the switch at all!

It really is that simple. Mapping Across works. I hope that you will see the importance in this technique and apply it to your own weight loss program. It has a wide variety of uses and will have a huge impact on your state of mind!

BEHAVIOR CREATOR

"When you fail to prepare, prepare to fail." Taking the time to set things up for yourself before you jump into a new, healthy, fit lifestyle is of the utmost importance. Mental imagery techniques allow us to lay the ground work that will help us to successfully achieve our weight loss goals and live a healthy lifestyle.

I found mental imagery helpful in making sure that I did not skip meals. I had heard that it was very important to eat 5 or 6 mini-meals throughout the day, and I had issues even sticking to 3. Others have used mental imagery to motivate themselves to work out harder and more often. I encourage you to use mental imagery to change whatever behavior it is that you believe will make a large impact on your weight loss program. Keep in mind though that more often than not little changes can have a powerful effect.

There are many types of mental imagery techniques, but the Behavior Creator will help with many issues that you have, or events that you might like to prevent, while getting started on your weight loss venture. It will help you to enact a new behavior subconsciously so that you do not have to expend energy *consciously* making a continual effort. You be able to operate more efficiently this way.

If we want new behaviors to stick around, we must connect the behavior to the outcome that we desire; which in this case is weight loss. If we can connect the end result with a new behavior, it is easier to keep it going. Here is how you can create a new behavior that will ensure your success in your weight loss program.

1. Choose a type of behavior that you want to develop. Pick one that is going to help you achieve your fitness goals. For me, it was to make sure that I ate many meals throughout the day. Others have decided to make exercise their focus. Do what works best for you.

2. Create a visualization of the behavior and how a situation might play out while you are engaged in it. See yourself fully engaged in the newly created behavior. Watch the visualization as if you were watching a movie. You can be the star, or watch someone else performing the said action that you have created. Use your

imagination and make the scene your own. Observe every detail.

3. If you are visualizing someone else engaging in this behavior, put yourself into their role. After watching them play the part, take over and observe yourself participating from an outside perspective.

4. Now, feel yourself behaving in such a manner. How is your body moving? What muscles are you using? Are you tense or relaxed? What is your posture like?

We must test this behavior to make sure it works and is really instilled into our subconscious.

1. Create 4 scenarios in your mind where this behavior will be of use. These situations should be ones that would have normally prompted your old behavior.

2. Place yourself in the scene. Sense everything that is going on around you. You are there in the moment. Take note of everything that is being picked up by your 5 senses.

3. Did your behavior change this time? Did you engage in your new behavior as opposed to your old, unwanted behavior? If you are still stuck in your old behavior, repeat the steps above to solidify the new behavior. Keep testing until you automatically use your newly created behavior.

CHAPTER 3 NLP During Your Weight Loss Program

Thanks to a boosted motivation level, I was on my way to the "new me." At the beginning of the process I realized that every day I felt as if I was battling my old eating habits. I would over eat. Consuming more calories than I was burning was stifling my goal. Eating the wrong foods was also keeping me from achieving physical wellbeing. I used a specific technique to change my bad eating habits. It is referred to as the Swish Pattern.

The Swish Pattern is a useful tool in changing old bad habits easily. It is a technique where you replace an undesirable habit for one you would prefer to have. I wanted to replace my unhealthy eating habits (junk food and over-eating) with healthy eating habits (energy foods and eating healthy portions). This tool helped me to change my thoughts and thought process regarding these habits, which in turn changed the bad behavior.

SWISH PATTERN

First, choose the habit/behavior that you desire to replace. Visualize it in your mind. Be in the moment of acting out this behavior. Use your five senses to recognize exactly what it feels like. What emotions do you have? Isolate a certain, vividly detailed image of yourself in the midst of engaging in this habit. For me, it was imagining myself shoving pizza into my mouth. Make sure you recognize that /this is something you have done in the past and that you want to keep it there. Take a mental picture.

Next, using all of your senses again, create another image of yourself being successful by replacing that bad eating habit with a healthy one. This will be your replacement snap shot. It is vivid, intense, and vibrant. In mine, I had eaten well and used proper portions. I was healthy and energized thanks to making good choices in regard to food. I stepped outside of this picture to see myself in it. At the bottom corner of the new image, you will place a tiny version of yourself in the midst of your bad habit. This tiny picture is dark and colorless.

A Healthy and Balanced Meal or...

Indulging in Unhealthy Habits...?

Now, re-visualize the first picture, the old you. At the bottom corner, darken the future picture (of you and your replacement behavior) and make it small. You can still see it but it is darker. Put yourself back into the poor emotional state that you are currently in. This is currently the big image. You should be feeling all of the self-defeating emotions associated with your bad habit like disappointment and self-loathing. Fully connect yourself with that moment.

Next, instantaneously switch the two images. Bring back the "new you," with your replacement behavior. Make it huge and colorful, full of everything to stimulate your senses. Shrink the picture of your unwanted behavior at the same time, moving it back into the corner and darken it. When you do this, make a "swwwwwisssssssshhhhhhhhh" sound. As I did this I would mentally jump into the replacement behavior image. The picture of you in the future is now the present. The old behavior is in the past, exactly where you want it to be.

I repeated this several times. Switching the pictures and jumping into my new behavioral image while "swooshing." Gradually increase the speed of the switch. Each time I was doing it faster and faster. Eventually it will become instantaneous. Replacing your bad eating habit will be as simple as that.

SETTING AN ANCHOR

Another Neuro-linguistic Programming technique I used on a consistent basis during my weight loss journey was Anchoring. Setting an anchor was immensely beneficial to me and I hope that it is for you as well. It helped me to get back the feeling of being motivated, healthy and happy like I used to be when I was in shape and healthy years ago. This technique helped to keep me driven during my weight loss program. The beauty of this process is that if one anchor does not produce the results you are looking for, it can always be replaced.

Anchoring Facts:

- They can be produced artificially or naturally (due to events).

- They can occur because of a single emotionally charged event or subconsciously through repetition, for example: advertising.

- Needs to be repeated; it can fade with time.

- Make sure you set the anchor when the feeling you want to reinforce is at its peak.

- Choose a very intense memory.

- Make sure that the stimulus you are using is as exclusive as possible. Don't use something you do all of the time.

- I stacked (set) my anchors for approximately 30 minutes; the longer the duration of repetition the better.

1. Choosing a memory- I remembered a time I was at the gym and was asked to be a trainer because I was at my physical best. You choose your own. Make sure it was emotionally intense.

2. Reliving the memory- Associate yourself with the memory. Be in that moment and see it through your own eyes. This made my feelings more intense. I made the picture of the event extremely colorful, large and bright. I intensified my feelings to the maximum.

3. Anchoring the memory- When I felt my emotions at their peak, I pinched the back of my hand. That was my trigger. You can do whatever works best for you: rub your earlobe, grab your knee, etc.

4. Stop at your peak- Release your trigger when your emotion peaks. I had to practice this step a few times before I had it down.

5. Testing the trigger/anchor- I stopped for a while and thought about something else, then used my trigger. If anchoring was successful, it will bring you directly back to that lovely emotional state immediately.

6. Repeat. - Repeat this several times. To make my anchor stronger and more powerful, I set 3-4

memories of times when I felt the same way to that identical trigger.

Anchoring was the most effective way to put myself in a motivated, positive mind set during my weight loss program. I used it almost every day, throughout the day. My trigger helped me be able to feel awesome and driven on demand. What better way to make it through a weight loss program?

SELF-CHECK

An additional way I used NLP ideas in my weight loss program was to check in with myself every day. I needed to make sure that I was staying on track. I would think about and ask myself these key questions:

1. What do I desire?
2. How will getting that help me?
3. What obstacles are keeping me from getting it?

4. What is essential to me?
5. What is working best in this situation?
6. What could be enhanced?
7. What resources am I going to utilize?

Self-evaluation is necessary to achieve any goal. Success in the short or long term requires that questions be asked and answers be evaluated. Then, if necessary, redirection must occur.

DISENGAGING A COMPULSION

I, as many people do, suffered from an eating disorder that some people do not recognize as one. Binge eating was a serious issue for me. I would engorge myself and end up feeling sick, physically and emotionally. I would feel great while I was committing the crime, but the aftermath left me feeling disgusting. I always hated myself afterward.

I used the following steps to break myself of this horrible compulsion. It worked very well for me. I have not fallen into doing it again thanks to this very beneficial process.

- First, I figured out what type of food I liked to binge on. For me, it was fast food; any type of fast food. For some it may be candy, carbs, etc.

- Next, I focused on the situation in which I would normally use this behavior. For me it was at the end of the month after working long hours. I would use it to reward myself, but it was really a punishment of sorts. Actually, it got so bad that I would automatically do it without even thinking about it. You must figure out in what situations you tend to binge.

- Picture the circumstances in your mind. Use your five senses to notice what is going on around you. I paid special attention to the actual food I was eating. Details are key.

- Clear your mind of the entire scene for a few moments. I would imagine a blank blue screen.

- Imagine next something that repulses you. For me, it was a decaying dead animal with maggots all over it. It can be garbage, vomit, or feces; anything that makes you sick. Imagine the taste and smell of it in your mouth. I would feel as though I was going to vomit. I used all of my senses again in this exercise. See it, smell it, hear it, taste it, and feel it.

- Remove the image from your mind once again and go back to imagining your binging situation. During your session this time, notice how pleasurable it is. When you take a bite this time around, you should notice that the sense of tasting something horrible has overwhelmed you. Exactly like when you were experiencing whatever it is that disgusts you.

- Do this five to ten times.

- Clear your mind once again for a few moments.

- Finally, imagine binging on your favorite food. This round should not bring about the same pleasure and desire. Personally, I just felt sick. I was experiencing the negative emotions I had in regard to the dead animal while picturing myself eating pizza; that which used to bring me pleasure.

I was able to be successful in disengaging my compulsive, automatic binge eating by using this method. It was a relief to never have to feel out of control again. I was cured and felt empowered once more.

COGNITIVE REFRAMING

Sometimes we make things more difficult for ourselves than they need to be. If we just take a little time and change our words for certain things, sometimes we can change our entire thought process. When we use Cognitive Reframing, we are choosing to cut off a negative way of thinking and talking; replacing these thoughts, phrases, and words with more positive ones. This not only works for weight loss and exercise regimes, but has been proven effective in many other areas. Even major corporations have used this method in dealing with customers and employees.

When used to your advantage, Cognitive Reframing can help you to turn a situation where you do not feel empowered into a moment of empowerment. This is a perfect way to change the way you think about weight loss and food, while in the midst of your program. Come up with your own language for your weight loss *journey*... see what I did there. It is that easy!

When you have a weight loss program that you are implementing, it is easy to get stressed out. Any major change in life can bring stress, but a new weight loss routine can be very intense because we are changing our entire lifestyle. We are causing stress to our mind and our bodies. We are basically shocking our entire system and it is very taxing. It is this stress that we put on ourselves that will usually thwart our weight loss efforts, not laziness or hunger. Cutting carbs, calories, and exerting extra physical energy by working out is physically and mentally demanding for anyone; from the beginner to the experienced.

Here are some more idea to get you started:
- "Calorie counting" BECOMES "Meal design"

- "Cheat day/cheat meal" BECOMES "Flexible eating plan/plateau breaker"
- "Diet" BECOMES "Modified eating regimen"
- "Difficult workout" BECOMES "High intensity"
- "Weight lifting" BECOMES "Strength training"
- "Will-power" BECOMES "Skill-power"
- "Lose weight" BECOMES "Burn fat"

As you can see, it really is that easy! Here are some steps you can take to come up with your own positive language and reframe your own thinking:

1. **Do a little research.** Figure out what negative thought processes you have in regard to your weight loss. Learn how pessimists see things. Read up on negative and positive explanatory thinking. It will help you to figure out what to change in order to have a more positive outlook so that you can keep stress to a minimum.

2. **Pay attention to what and how you are thinking.** Observe when you become stressed and what negative thoughts you might be experiencing at the time. Being mindful about what you are thinking can help. See your thoughts and thought processes from the outside; observe your own thinking. You will get better and better at sensing these thoughts when they first come to mind. Then, you can start to turn them around when they come about. You will go from negative to positive thinking easily with just a little bit of practice. Soon it will be effort less, and you will find losing weight to be much less stressful!

3. **Now that you are aware of your negative thought processes in regard to weight loss, test them.** A major component of reframing requires us to check for the validity of our thoughts. Are they real? Are they true? If they are, figure out a more positive way to look at what is happening. No, you are not lying to

yourself. You will simply be seeing things more positively, allowing you to have a less stressful experience in general. Constantly try to see things differently, in a more positive light.

4. **Now it is time to consciously switch your thoughts.** Now that you: know the effects of negative and how they affect your stress levels, are able to label negative thoughts as they arise, have checked to make sure they are valid, and have looked at weight loss in a more positive way, it is time to switch your thoughts. Any negative thoughts that you have in regard to your weight loss program can bring about negative emotions and stress. Simply come up with new key phrases that are positive to replace the old, negative ones. The more you use this new motivating, uplifting language, the less stressful and more positive your weight loss journey will be! It really is all in your head!

LAST STRAW METHOD

In order to pursue a goal, especially an all-encompassing or difficult one, we need motivation. Motivation not only gives us a jump start that we need to begin achieving our goals, it also is the main thing that keeps us going in the right direction during the process. This technique helps us to take an unpleasant emotion or habit and blow it up until we cannot tolerate it any longer. It makes you feel like, "ENOUGH IS ENOUGH!!" This method really helped me to put my foot down… with myself.

This method helps us to take something that is not healthy or positive, and say, "I have had enough!" Get rid of things that are not in your best interest with this technique. Most of us are guilty of tolerating things that we should not just because they may not be detrimental to our existence. In regard to weight loss, this could be midnight binging on cookies. It could be the soda on our break at work, or the occasional de-stressing cigarette. Yet, even though these things are not good for us, they are not unendurable. A lot of the time we need an insufferable circumstance in order to put an end to it.

This is where the Last Straw Method is useful. It allows us to alter our thinking and make our mind believe that the situation or habit has become unbearable. This is known as a threshold pattern. We must not only get to the threshold, we must go over it.

Here is an example of reaching your threshold: After binging on pizza all night, the night before, you woke up disappointed in yourself and appalled by your own behavior. Yet, you did not stop the binging. Two days later you polished off a gallon of ice cream and a 2 lb bag of fries.

Here is an example of going over your threshold: Your boyfriend calls you fat and "moos" every time you eat. You are distraught and dump him.

Here is put the Last Straw Method into practice:

Visualize a situation when you were *at* your threshold, but did not go over it.

As the intensity of the situation builds, take note of all the details that you can. Are noises becoming slowly louder or quieter? Is the picture of the situation getting larger, smaller, dimmer, or brighter? How is the vision changing as the tension is building?

Now, visualize a situation where you went *over* the threshold. Usually the visualization will undergo a massive change when you cross the threshold. Did you see another picture that was very different from the one you saw before crossing the threshold? Did you hear self-talk saying "I'm done" or "no more?" How did you look? Did you appear happier or more self-assured?

The last thing that you need to do is apply the feelings and sensory information that you picked up on in your "crossing the threshold" scenario, and apply them to your "reaching the threshold" scenario. Visualize the whole scene differently, with more confidence.

Push yourself over the edge and never deal with the same issue again! Repeat as many times as you need to in order to feel that, "ENOUGH IS ENOUGH!"

FUTURE PACING

One of the best ways that I have found to curb my appetite using NLP, is through Future Pacing. In this technique, we use mental pictures and visualizations (I think of them as movies in my head) to make changes in ourselves that we will need to access in the future. We can use anchors to bring about the new feeling when needed.

We can test this technique by triggering the anchor and seeing if the newly programmed thought or idea kicks in. It should arise automatically. Here is a practical, easy way to use this technique:

Visualize yourself in a situation where you want to engage in a certain behavior or would like to end up with a certain outcome. For me I chose being at a party with a lot of high calorie snacks, high fat deserts and h'ordeuvres, and drinks. I do not eat any of them.

Not only because I have self-control, but because I was just not hungry!! Pretend like you are watching a movie. What are you wearing, doing, and saying? What smells do you smell? How do you sound? As I stayed away from the no-no foods, I was confident. I could see it in my posture and the way I walked. I was not shaken by the food.

Now, jump into the picture and experience the situation first hand. What can you hear, see, and feel? Note everything about the experience you are having while utilizing your new trait.

When you feel the new behavior peak, or become the strongest, use a physical trigger and anchor the feeling to it. I usually tap my palm, but do whatever works best for you.

Practice and relate your new characteristic to all of the sensory information that you picked up while visualizing the scenario playing out in your head. All of the things that you saw, smelled, felt, heard, etc., should now bring about the new behavior or emotion that you wanted to enact within yourself. Do not forget to use your trigger. After rehearsing many times, anchoring the feeling, and observing everything around you with all of your senses, you experience this new conduct in real life situations, exactly how you experienced it in your visualization.

COMPULSION BLOWOUT TECHNIQUE

Do you have a compulsion that you feel might be out of your control? Is this behavior inhibiting your weight loss in any way? If so, the Compulsion Blowout Technique may be the perfect option to help you get rid of unnecessary, compulsive behavior.

This technique worked perfectly for me. I used it to rid myself of my chocolate "addiction." Anytime I thought of chocolate, smelled chocolate, or saw chocolate, I ate it. Even my co-workers' candy dishes and my son's Halloween stash were not safe from my compulsive chocolate eating. Today, I am in control.

Not that I *never* eat chocolate, but I dictate when and where I consume it. Here is how you can join me in beating compulsive behavior:

Picture the one thing you have a huge weakness for: smoking, fatty foods, carbs, candy, etc. Pay attention to where this mental picture is in your mind. Is it directly in the middle of your mind? Is it near, far, to the left, or to the right? How large is it?

Now picture one thing that relates to a behavior that is non-compulsive for you. For example, taking vitamins, or brushing your hair. Where is the image? What size is it? Ask yourself the same questions as in number one and note your answers.

If it is helpful for you, list all of the answers on a piece of paper. One set for the thing that represents your compulsion and the other for the non-compulsive image. List the differences in what you see and hear. Note the dissimilarities.

Now, start playing around with the image in your mind related to your compulsive behavior. You want to increase the size, location, or sounds related to that image. For instance, if the size of the image is a lot larger than the other, keep blowing it up in your mind until it is so undeniably huge that it is no longer a compulsion for you. You want the image to morph into one that is absolutely ridiculous. If there is a sound involved, turn up the volume in your mind until it seems to blow out your eardrums. This will disallow the compulsive behavior from having any control over you anymore. Say you see a chocolate bar, blow it up until it is so large that you get a stomach ache just visualizing it.

Do this quite a few times, in the same exact manner. Take breaks, but go back to the same process. Visualize it, and then quickly exaggerate!

Test your method and see if the change sticks. With a little work it will. Soon enough, your mind will switch up the image automatically and you will not fall victim to your compulsion anymore!

CHAPTER 4 NLP to Maintain Weight Loss Success

Once I achieved victory in losing weight through diet and exercise, I realized that I still had one more part to my goal. I wanted to be successful in maintaining the "new me." In evaluating this secondary goal, I realized that it was actually just as challenging, if not more difficult than successfully losing the weight in the first place.

Maintaining a healthier, thinner self is a long, slow process. Self-control is used on a regular basis and motivation must always be there to exercise. I was happy with myself, and that helped to encourage me. The amount of time that I had spent implementing and developing new habits was also advantageous in retaining my weight loss. Yet, because I had lost weight years before and gained it back, I knew the possibility of it happening again would always be there.

This time around, I took an extra step to ensure my long-term weight loss success. Neuro-linguistic Programming helped me to make certain that I would not gain weight again. It was extremely beneficial to continue utilizing the same tools I used during my program of weight loss to maintain my newfound health and figure. The same tools that helped me to drop the pounds assisted me in keeping them off. I added one more technique to my arsenal to make sure that I would be able to maintain my lighter, healthier self: a Well Formed Outcome.

A Well Formed Outcome helped me to keep the weight off by reminding me of and helping me to focus on my goal. My goal was to be lean and healthy, not just to lose weight and end up gaining it again. Sure, I had been triumphant in dropping the pounds. However, by having a Well Formed Outcome, I was able to ensure that I would stay motivated for the long-term in order to stay leaner and healthy.

Well Formed Outcomes are usually developed when you begin pursuing a goal. Yet, it is also what will keep you going until the end. It will aid you and be a driving force in staying successful when used as a long-term motivation tool.

Here are some tips that I used to create my Well Formed Outcome:

1) Understand *what* you want, not what you *do not* want.

Goals must have a positive focus. Instead of wanting to lose weight or not be fat; a better goal would be, "I would like to be healthy and trim." Focus on something you want to have instead of what you would like to stay away from.

2) Have a decent time frame.

Give yourself enough time to get the job done. Do not be too vague. Saying that I would like to lose 30 pounds as soon as possible might have been too overwhelming for me. Deciding to be healthy and trim is great, but without a time frame at all, it would have been harder to track and monitor my progress. "I would like to become healthy and trim in a year and stay that way for the rest of my life." This goal is both positive and gives a decent amount of time to accomplish that it.

3) Make sure to take full responsibility.

I was solely responsible for my outcome. No one else can be used as an excuse for why goals cannot be reached. This is not to say that you may not need help along the way, but no one else can be blamed for failure.

4) Focus and be specific with your outcome.

Utilizing all of my senses, I sat down and focused. I wrote out in detail how I would feel once I achieved my goal. The more specific that the details are, the more powerful the aspiration to succeed will be.

5) What resources are necessary to be successful and reach the objective?

What information will I need? What gear must I buy? What other resources can help me to reach my goal? These are all important questions to note and answer. Knowing where I wanted to go and how I was going to get there helped to motivate me.

6) Go over your goals on a regular basis.

Goals must be imbedded into the subconscious. Remember, the subconscious cannot tell when something is an actual event or when it is imaginary. Everyday feel your future success as if you are already there experiencing it for yourself.

Adapting the techniques that I used during my weight loss program to my maintenance program helped me to hold on to my thinner self. Additionally, creating my future success and reliving it in my mind everyday was a powerful tool in maintaining my weight loss. I was able to concentrate on being fit and healthy, instead of falling back into negative behaviors. I am still incredibly motivated five years later, all thanks to Neuro-linguistic Programming methods.

CONCLUSION

Thank you again for purchasing this book!

I hope this book was able to help you see that Neuro-linguistic Programming is an immensely useful field of study that will enable you to reach your weight loss goals. Disappointment and shame will be a thing of the past. Achievement is in your future, do not delay. The "new you" is waiting!

Staying healthy is the most important thing that you can do for yourself. It takes motivation, will power and hard work but is a most rewarding venture to undertake. Most people do not realize that it is the power of the mind that controls the body. Harness and redirect the power of yours. Literally, it is all in your head.

Imagine never "yo-yo" dieting again. Picture yourself desiring to go to the gym and enjoying working out. Your imagination will be a driving force in helping you reach these goals. I know my mother would always tell me to use my imagination as a child, but I never thought it could be such a mighty tool.

NLP has helped many people to be successful, and it helped me to reach my goals as well. NLP is a vital tool for anyone who is trying to lose weight. How can you go wrong using techniques derived from "the study of success?" Failure will no longer be an option.

I wish you well on your quest to lose weight. You can do it! I did.

Finally, I would like to ask you to do me a little favor and comment on my book on Amazon.

Thank you and good luck with your NLP journey!

James

Connect with me and other authors at:

www.facebook.com/HolisticWellnessBooks

www.twitter.com/Wellness_Books

Free Complimentary eBook

Download it at:

www.bitly.com/alkapaleofree

Recommended Reading

James Adler's Books

Success Secrets: Change Your Life With Neuro-Linguistic Programming. NLP Techniques for Personal and Professional Success and Lifestyle Transformation

Feng Shui For Wellness and Wealth

To find similar books related to health, personal development and spirituality, visit:

www.HolisticWellnessBooks.com